Original title:
Glistening Pines

Copyright © 2024 Swan Charm
All rights reserved.

Author: Liisi Lendorav
ISBN HARDBACK: 978-9916-79-774-7
ISBN PAPERBACK: 978-9916-79-775-4
ISBN EBOOK: 978-9916-79-776-1

Serenity Cloaked in Evergreen Hues

In a glade where shadows play,
Whispers soft at break of day.
Emerald canopies stretch wide,
Peaceful dreams where hearts can bide.

Gentle breezes kiss the leaves,
Nature's song, the spirit weaves.
Time slows down in tranquil grace,
A hidden world, a serene space.

Murmurs of the Leafy Charms

Rustling leaves in soft embrace,
Echo laughter, nature's trace.
Each branch a tale, a story spun,
In leafy whispers, life begun.

Cascading light in golden streams,
Dance of shadows, woven dreams.
Hearts entwined with nature's chord,
Murmurs sweet, a soft accord.

A Symphony of Twinkling Pines

Underneath the twinkling stars,
Pines stand tall, like ancient bars.
Melodies of crickets play,
Nighttime's serenade, a sway.

The moonlight glimmers on the trunks,
Every sound, a spark, it plunks.
Nature's choir in rhythmic charms,
Lost in night, we find our arms.

Luminary Twilight in the Thicket

Twilight drapes a soft, warm veil,
Cascades of light, a gentle trail.
Thicket alive with whispered calls,
Embers glow as the darkness falls.

In shadows deep, the secrets lay,
Softly spoken, they sway and play.
A tranquil heart finds peace so bright,
In luminary twilight's light.

The Allure of Nature's Crystal Veils

In morning light, the dew does gleam,
A thousand pearls, like dreams they seem.
Nested in grass, a soft embrace,
Nature's jewels in a silent race.

Whispers of winds through trees they play,
Dancing leaves in a golden sway.
With each breeze, stories unfold,
Of ancient secrets, softly told.

The brook's laughter, a soothing sound,
In glistening ripples, solace found.
Over pebbles, it twists and turns,
Nature's melody, the heart it churns.

Mountains loom, their crowns of white,
Guardians of the day and night.
Veils of mist, in shadows draped,
Whispering tales of life, escaped.

Beneath the stars, the world anew,
Soft murmurs rise, of night's debut.
With every breath, the earth reveals,
The wondrous charm of crystal veils.

Crystal Dreams Underneath the Trees

Beneath the canopy so wide,
Crystal dreams in silence hide.
Whispers float on gentle breeze,
Secrets shared among the leaves.

Soft light filters through the green,
Dancing shadows, bright and serene.
Nature's world, a sacred place,
In this moment, time slows its race.

Mossy beds where visions gleam,
Life awakens in the dream.
Branches cradle all our thoughts,
In their arms, we're never lost.

Raindrops fall like sparkling stars,
Nature's magic, healing scars.
Every sigh, a fleeting chance,
In the woods, our spirits dance.

Here in this enchanted glade,
Where our worries start to fade.
Crystal dreams beneath the trees,
Whisper tales on fragrant breeze.

Whispers of Needle and Light

In the forest, secrets sigh,
Whispers of needle and light.
Sunbeams filter, soft and bright,
Nature's song, a pure delight.

Branches sway in rhythmic tune,
Underneath the watchful moon.
Silhouette of dreams taking flight,
Echoes linger in the night.

Dewdrops glisten on the leaves,
Carpet where the spirit weaves.
Every path a story told,
As the night begins to fold.

Beneath the stars, life's embrace,
Whispers float in sacred space.
Each soft rustle, every sound,
Rooted hopes in earth unbound.

Feeling magic in the air,
In this world, we are laid bare.
Whispers of needle and light,
Guide us through the velvet night.

Shadows of Evergreen Dreams

In the grove where shadows play,
Evergreen dreams drift away.
Nature holds with gentle hands,
Silent magic in the sands.

Twilight weaves a story old,
Wrapped in whispers, brave and bold.
Misty paths of emerald hue,
Lead the heart where dreams come true.

Songs of crickets fill the air,
Softly calling souls laid bare.
Every rustle, every sound,
Navigates the heart profound.

Lush terrain where memories grow,
In the twilight's gentle glow.
Shadows dance, a mystic seam,
Stitching together our dream.

Underneath the starlit dome,
In this wild, I feel at home.
Shadows of evergreen dreams,
Where the heart forever gleams.

Treetops Kissing the Dawn

As the sun begins to rise,
Treetops kiss the morning skies.
Golden light ignites the day,
Painting pathways in bright array.

Whispers of the waking earth,
Celebrate the hour of birth.
Every leaf a radiant smile,
Nature's beauty to beguile.

Crickets hush, the world anew,
Colors dance in every hue.
Buds unfurl, the blossoms bloom,
Filling air with sweet perfume.

Skyward calls the lark and thrush,
In each breath, a soft warm hush.
Treetops sway in gentle song,
Where the heart feels it belongs.

In the glow of dawn's embrace,
Life unfolds at its own pace.
Treetops kissing the dawn's light,
Guiding dreams through day and night.

Gleams of Solitude in the Pines

In the quiet grove, shadows sway,
Sunlight filters, soft and gray.
Whispers linger, secrets unfold,
Nature's stories quietly told.

Among the trunks, a breeze will sigh,
Echoes of laughter, long gone by.
Each needle glistens, a gentle dance,
In the pines, we find our trance.

Footsteps muffled on the pine-needled floor,
Every heartbeat, we yearn for more.
Through branches high, the sky peeks in,
A world beyond where our thoughts begin.

Underneath the boughs, time stands still,
Moments captured, a tranquil thrill.
In the solitude, peace intertwines,
Here in the heart of the whispering pines.

The Glow of Whispering Winds

Gentle breezes trace the hills,
Carrying tales with subtle thrills.
They dance through meadows, across the lake,
In their embrace, heartbeats awake.

Over the valleys, their song does weave,
A melody captured, none can believe.
With every sigh, the grasses bend,
In whispers soft, they start to blend.

Through tangled woods, secrets fly,
As shadows stretch and dreams comply.
The whispering winds weave through the night,
An endless journey, a delicate flight.

Touched by moonlight, they softly glow,
Guiding us places we long to go.
In their arms, the world feels right,
Whispers become the stars' delight.

Mirrored Moments in Tall Boughs

In the forest, reflections gleam,
Tall boughs cradle our waking dream.
Each moment captured, still and bright,
Nature's canvas in fading light.

Beneath the canopy, echoes blend,
Stories of old that never end.
Leaves shimmer softly, dancing free,
In every rustle, a memory.

Time suspended, as shadows play,
Lost in the weave of the day.
In mirrored moments, two worlds meet,
Life's reflections at our feet.

Through the branches, sunlight streams,
Filling hearts with gentle dreams.
In the stillness, peace surrounds,
Mirrored laughter, love abounds.

Hidden Gems of the Quiet Thicket

In the thicket, treasures lie,
Soft whispers of nature brush by.
Shadows hide in a leafy embrace,
Secrets waiting to leave their trace.

Among the ferns, the wildflowers bloom,
Colors burst forth, dispelling gloom.
Each petal glistens with morning dew,
Hidden gems, a world anew.

Beneath the branches, soft and low,
Lives a world few dare to know.
In the silence, a heartbeat sings,
Life's simple joy, the thicket brings.

Rustling leaves weave stories untold,
In the quiet thicket, mysteries unfold.
With every step on this hallowed ground,
Hidden gems of nature abound.

Ethereal Rays in the Woodland

Sunbeams dance through leaves, bright,
Whispers of dawn, soft and light.
Gentle breezes weave their song,
In this haven, where dreams belong.

Mossy carpets, emerald green,
Nature's treasures, rarely seen.
Fallen branches, tales they tell,
Of ancient spirits that bid farewell.

Dappled shadows on the ground,
Magic lies all around.
Every rustle, every sigh,
Echoes of life gently nigh.

Flickering lights, the fireflies,
Guide the wanderers' wistful eyes.
In the quiet, heartbeats blend,
With the woodland, we transcend.

Paths unfold in mystic ways,
Amidst the beauty, time decays.
Ethereal rays, a fleeting sight,
Kissing the earth with pure delight.

Luminous Trails Through the Timberland

Moonlight drapes the forest's skin,
A silver path where dreams begin.
Each step whispers ancient lore,
Of wandering souls from times of yore.

Tall trees rise, a sacred choir,
Bathed in glow, they never tire.
Branches sway, a gentle hymn,
In this realm, we lose and win.

Stars peer through in eager thrall,
Guiding hearts that heed their call.
Trailing light, where shadows creep,
Secrets in the night, they keep.

Soft reflections on the stream,
Woven gently, like a dream.
Nature's canvas, bright and wide,
Luminous trails, we glide inside.

Every moment, still and bright,
In the timber, pure delight.
Luminous paths, both wild and free,
Reveal the world's deep mystery.

Illuminated Journeys in Silvan Realms

Beneath the canopy so grand,
Whispers linger, hand in hand.
Illuminated trails we seek,
In the silence, nature speaks.

Golden hues of twilight blaze,
Transforming woodlands in a haze.
Every corner holds a tale,
Of enchanted winds that softly sail.

Among the ferns, soft and lush,
In our hearts, there stirs a rush.
Illumination, pure and clear,
Guides our paths, dispelling fear.

With each step, a new embrace,
Magic woven in this space.
Silvan realms, where dreams reside,
In their light, we take our stride.

Journeys crafted with such care,
In this wonder, none compare.
Together, through the night we roam,
In illuminated woods, our home.

A Symphony of Light Among the Pines

Among the pines, a serenade,
Where light and shadow interplay.
Gentle whispers, a melodic flow,
In harmonious grace, we glow.

Sunbeams strum the needles fine,
Creating songs that brightly shine.
Rustling bristles sway with grace,
In nature's concert, find our place.

Golden rays through branches chase,
In this enchanted, wooded space.
Notes of wind, a symphony,
We dance in tune with the melody.

Each moment holds a fleeting beat,
As we find joy in simple feats.
A tapestry of light and sound,
In this haven, peace is found.

In the stillness, hearts entwine,
A symphony of light divine.
Among the pines, forever blessed,
Together, in this light, we rest.

A Tapestry of Light and Life

In the dawn's gentle glow,
Colors blend and shift,
Whispers of the morning,
Nature's tender gift.

Petals dance with the breeze,
Sunlight weaves a song,
Life awakens softly,
In harmony, we belong.

Rivers rippling with dreams,
Flowing through the land,
Every turn a blessing,
Crafted by nature's hand.

Mountains stand in silence,
Guardians of the day,
Beneath their watchful gaze,
We find our way and play.

Stars begin their twinkle,
As night unfolds its grace,
A tapestry of wonder,
In this enchanted place.

The Resounding Echoes of the Forest

Whispering leaves above,
In symphony with the ground,
Echoes of the ancients,
In every sight and sound.

Footsteps softly tread,
On paths both old and wise,
Stories wrapped in shadows,
Beneath the vast, blue skies.

Moss carpets the earth,
In hues of vibrant green,
A cradle for the creatures,
In this tranquil scene.

Branches reach for the light,
Woven in a dance,
Nature sings its verses,
In every glance.

With each step, a heartbeat,
In this sacred space,
The forest's rhythm guides us,
With its warm embrace.

Bejeweled Embrace of Ancient Trees

In the twilight's soft glow,
Ancient trees will stand tall,
Their branches like wide arms,
Inviting us to fall.

Leaves adorned with diamonds,
In the evening's soft breeze,
Each whisper tells a story,
Of love between the trees.

Roots deep in the soil,
Carrying tales untold,
Of seasons that have passed,
And moments pure as gold.

The canopy above,
A shelter from the night,
In their bejeweled embrace,
We find our heart's delight.

Beneath their wise shadows,
We pause, reflect, and dream,
In nature's gentle cradle,
Life flows like a stream.

Serenity in the Sparkling Shade

In the cool, gentle shade,
Where the sunlight plays,
Nature's calm surrounds us,
In a tranquil haze.

Birds sing a soft lullaby,
Notes drifting on the air,
Beneath the verdant boughs,
We find solace rare.

Dappled light falls softly,
On faces filled with peace,
Here in this moment,
All worries seem to cease.

The rustle of the leaves,
Like whispers from above,
In the sparkling shade,
We awaken to love.

Time slows in this haven,
Where hearts can gently mend,
In nature's sweet embrace,
We find our journey's end.

The Glittering Hush of Tall Pines

In the stillness of the night,
Whispers sway with gentle grace.
Tall pines stand like sentinels,
Guarding secrets time will trace.

Moonlight glimmers on each bough,
Casting shadows, soft and deep.
Nature breathes a whispered vow,
In her arms, the world will sleep.

Crickets sing a lullaby,
Echoes fill the quiet air.
Stars above like watchful eyes,
Gaze down with a knowing stare.

Breeze caresses rugged bark,
Guiding dreams where peace ignites.
In the pines, a sacred spark,
Illuminates the tranquil nights.

Every twig and leaf in tune,
Swaying softly, heartbeats blend.
In the glow of silver moon,
Magic weaves, no need to pretend.

A Celestial Tincture on Nature's Palette

Brush of dawn paints skies aglow,
Softest yellows, pinks, and blues.
Strokes of light begin to flow,
Waking earth from nightly snooze.

Each flower blooms in shades of dreams,
Colors bright, in joyful dance.
Nature's art, or so it seems,
Invites all to take a chance.

Leaves unfurl in emerald hues,
Breezes carry whispered lore.
In this canvas, hearts will choose,
To find beauty evermore.

Clouds weave cotton candy skies,
Swirling past the tall, green trees.
This vibrant world, it never lies,
In its splendor, souls find ease.

With each sunset, shades transform,
Burnished golds and fiery reds.
Nature paints in perfect form,
A masterpiece that never sheds.

Embers of Sunlight Dancing on Ferns

Morning sun in soft embrace,
Kisses ferns with golden light.
Each frond sways with gentle grace,
In this dance, a pure delight.

Shadows play on forest floor,
Patterns shift with each new breeze.
Nature's touch, we can't ignore,
Calls our hearts to feel at ease.

Every ray a fleeting spark,
Illuminates the quiet space.
Whispers float within the dark,
Drawing truth from nature's grace.

Time stands still in this embrace,
As sunlight weaves its golden thread.
In the warmth, we find our place,
Among the dreams that softly spread.

Ferns respond with tender sway,
Embers dance upon their fronds.
In this moment, lost in play,
Nature's song, our hearts respond.

Reflections of Dreams in Woodland Whispers

Deep in the woods where silence dwells,
Shadows hold the lore of time.
Whispers rise like soft-spun spells,
Carried on the breeze's chime.

Mossy carpets cradle thoughts,
Gentle sighs beneath the trees.
In each nook, a world begot,
Where dreams twine with nature's keys.

Sunlight finds its way through leaves,
Dancing on the forest floor.
In these woods, our spirit weaves,
Threads of beauty to explore.

Rippling streams like laughter flow,
Carving paths through ancient roots.
Here, the heart can freely show,
The quiet song that life computes.

Within this realm of timeless grace,
Reflections shimmer in the night.
Dreams linger in this sacred space,
Guiding souls to find their light.

The Quiet Dance of the Timbers

In the hush of the grove, whispers play,
Leaves flutter softly, in twilight's sway.
Bark creaks gently, a rhythmic old tune,
While shadows embrace the light of the moon.

Branches entwined, a graceful ballet,
Nature's sweet whispers guide night to day.
The stars twinkle down, a silent applause,
For each little movement, each rustle it draws.

Moss cloaks the ground, a velvety bed,
The timbers unite, where no words are said.
A tranquil ballet, amidst whispers and sighs,
A story of silence where true beauty lies.

Shadows Glinting in the Wilderness

In the heart of the jaunt, where shadows loom,
Whispers of secrets fill up the room.
Mist weaves around like a soft, silken veil,
Carrying stories of those who prevail.

Branches stretch high, like fingers reaching,
In nature's grand choir, the whispers are teaching.
Each rustle and murmur, a promise unheard,
The song of the wild, an undying word.

Crickets chirp lively, a rhythmic beat,
Stars sprinkle down, making night feel complete.
The shadows now dance in a flickering light,
And dreams take their flight on this magical night.

Enigma of the Woods at Dawn

As dawn breaks anew, colors softly bloom,
Mysteries linger, dispelling the gloom.
Soft whispers of night fade into the haze,
With each rustling leaf, the world starts to graze.

Fog wraps the ground in a gentle embrace,
Encouraging silence to set a slow pace.
Creatures retreat to their tucked-away homes,
While daylight reveals all that darkness shrouds.

The sunlight spills gold through the boughs overhead,
Awakening life where the shadows once led.
Each moment a puzzle, nature's grand scheme,
Wrapped in enigma, like a soft, radiant dream.

Luminescence in Tall Silences

In forests so deep, where echoes abide,
A luminescent glow, the soul's quiet guide.
Beneath ancient trees, where stillness is found,
Nature whispers softly, her secrets unbound.

Moonbeams cascade like silvered sighs,
Illuminating paths where the hidden heart lies.
Caught in the stillness, time seems to pause,
A moment of magic, just because.

Each step is a dance on this blanket of night,
With shadows that shimmer, pure and bright.
In tall, tender silences, life starts to gleam,
As the world finds solace in every shared dream.

Light Play on Pinecones' Tips

Sunlight dances on tips so bright,
Pinecones glisten, a joyful sight.
Nature's art in golden hues,
Whispers of beauty, the heart renews.

Shadows lengthen, twilight's call,
Pine trees sway, and then they fall.
Softly cradled, the forest sleeps,
In dreams of light, the silence creeps.

Dance of breezes through branches roam,
Each pinecone holds a tale of home.
Secrets shared in evening's glow,
A symphony only the trees know.

A Tapestry of Green and Gold

Fields stretch wide, a quilt of earth,
Emerald blades give nature birth.
Golden rays cascade and play,
Every hue defines the day.

Breezes weave through hanging leaves,
Whispered stories the forest weaves.
Patterns dance on sunlit ground,
In this tapestry, peace is found.

Moments linger, vibrant and bold,
Life's rich story silently told.
With every rustle, with every sigh,
Nature's heartbeats softly lie.

Veiled in Nature's Silken Touch

Dewdrops glisten, a silken veil,
Nature drapes its mystic tale.
Each petal soft, each leaf alive,
In the hush, the wild thrives.

Gentle whispers through the trees,
Carried forth by the playful breeze.
Nature's hands mold every form,
In her warmth, the weak grow warm.

A canvas brushed with tender grace,
Life unfurls in this sacred space.
Veils of mist, secrets to share,
In her silence, we find prayer.

Emerald Whispers of the Wild

Forest deep with shadows cast,
Emerald whispers, the die is cast.
Life unfolds beneath the trees,
In the rustle of hidden leaves.

Crickets sing their evening song,
In the wild, we all belong.
Moonlight kisses the fragrant air,
Secrets held, too sweet to share.

Nature's call, a soft embrace,
In her arms, time finds its grace.
Forever holds the stories spun,
Emerald tales beneath the sun.

Serene Days in a Hushed Glade

In quiet corners, shadows lay,
Soft whispers weave through leaves at play,
Sunlight dapples on the forest floor,
Each breath a melody, nature's score.

Golden hues in early morn's embrace,
Gentle breezes stir with tender grace,
Ferns unfurl as if to greet the dawn,
While time surrenders, ever drawn.

Birds take flight in graceful arcs above,
Chirping sweetly, a song of love,
Rustling branches, secrets softly share,
In every moment, magic fills the air.

Mossy carpets, emerald and bright,
Softly cradle footsteps, pure delight,
Cool shadows hide in the midday sun,
Serene days whisper, we are one.

As twilight falls and colors blend,
Stars emerge, a shimmering friend,
A hush descends, the world feels blessed,
In a glade of dreams, the heart finds rest.

Verdant Majesty Kissing the Sky

Beneath tall boughs, where the wild blooms thrive,
In emerald fields, the spirits come alive,
Each breath a testament to nature's grace,
A dance of colors, a warm embrace.

Mountains rise with majesty untold,
Whispers of stories in brown and gold,
Clouds drift softly like drifting dreams,
In this vast theater, beauty gleams.

Roots reach deep where the ancient's lie,
Connecting earth to the endless sky,
Rivers carve through, a silver thread,
Life unfolds in the paths it's led.

Sunsets paint the sky with fiery hues,
Day bids farewell, while night renews,
Stars twinkle bright, like diamonds spun,
In verdant realms, our hearts are one.

Each dawn brings promise, fresh and new,
Nature's canvas, forever in view,
An ode to majesty, evergreen sighs,
In whispers of love, we rise and fly.

Radiant Union of Earth and Air

In a world where the blue meets the green,
Harmony weaves through spaces unseen,
Mountains speak softly to the clouds,
As waves of wind form playful shrouds.

Sunlit meadows stretch far and wide,
A gentle breeze in nature's stride,
Blossoms excited to greet the dawn,
Each petal shines with a beauty withdrawn.

The symphony plays with rustling trees,
A melody carried upon the breeze,
Kites in the sky paint dreams anew,
Earth and air blend in vibrant hue.

Storm clouds gather, yet softly depart,
Bringing life anew to every heart,
Lightning flashes, a momentous spark,
In radiant union, igniting the dark.

At dusk, the horizon wears amber and gold,
Echoes of stories in silence unfold,
In this fleeting dance beneath the sky,
Earth and air whisper their sweet goodbye.

Flashes of Wonder in the Woodlands

In the heart of green, magic stands bold,
Every shadow a story waiting to unfold,
Dappled sunlight weaves tales of delight,
While wonders awaken, dissolving the night.

A flicker of wings, a darting sight,
Creatures at play, just out of light,
Mushrooms arise, gems in the shade,
Leading the wanderers, paths they've made.

Hidden nooks breathe fragrance so sweet,
Where time takes a pause, and all moments meet,
Chains of silence gently break,
As laughter and echoes start to wake.

Glistening dew upon the grass shines bright,
Mirroring stars in the soft twilight,
A gentle rustle, the forest sighs,
In flashes of wonder, the heart replies.

Moonbeams dance upon the forest floor,
Tales of the night whisper evermore,
With each step taken in the woodlands' embrace,
Magic surrounds us, a warm, soft trace.

A Forest Awash in Luminous Grace

In the dawn's embrace, shadows sway,
Whispers of breezes softly play.
Leaves glisten bright, a jeweled array,
Nature's symphony guides the way.

Morning dew clings to emerald green,
A tranquil world, so pure, serene.
Every step a dance, a gentle scene,
In this moment, all is unseen.

Sunlight trickles through the tall pines,
Where the air is sweet, pure like wines.
A hidden path where the heart aligns,
Each breath taken, divine designs.

Birds in chorus, their songs take flight,
Creatures awake, in soft morning light.
Underneath arches of nature's might,
The forest breathes, a wondrous sight.

Every glance, a treasure, a grace,
In this realm, time finds its place.
Hearts find solace in nature's space,
A forest awash in luminous grace.

Cascading Light Through Boughs

Golden rays kiss the forest floor,
A tapestry woven, forevermore.
Cascading light through boughs so sure,
Nature's artwork, an endless tour.

Shadows dance with each gentle breeze,
Rustling leaves sing sweet melodies.
In this haven, the soul finds ease,
Among the swaying ancient trees.

Filtered sunlight, a painter's brush,
Dappled patterns in a tender hush.
In the woodland's heart, we feel the rush,
Of love and peace, a sacred crush.

Every step, a path to explore,
Where magic lingers, spirits soar.
Cascading light, forever in store,
In this forest, we long for more.

Moments gather, like leaves in fall,
Nature's whispers, we hear the call.
Cascading light through branches tall,
In this realm, we find it all.

Ethereal Breaths of the Evergreen

In shadows deep, where silence hums,
Breath of the forest softly comes.
Ethereal whispers from the drums,
Of ancient trees, a life that thrums.

The scent of cedar, rich and pure,
Carries our hearts, a gentle lure.
Beneath the boughs, we find the cure,
In the embrace of nature's whir.

Misty trails through the twilight dim,
Voices of nature, a soothing hymn.
In the green depths, the light grows slim,
Ethereal breaths, where spirits swim.

The pine-scented air stirs the soul,
Bringing to light what makes us whole.
Among the branches, we lose control,
In this kingdom, we reach our goal.

With each heartbeat, the forest sings,
A dance of life, with all it brings.
Ethereal breaths, the joy it flings,
In the evergreen, our essence clings.

Golden Hues in a Woodland Reverie

Sunset spills warmth on woodland trails,
Golden hues light the shifting scales.
In this reverie, silence prevails,
As nature unfolds her timeless tales.

Crimson leaves fall, a gentle kiss,
Every glance brings a moment of bliss.
In this dream, we find our abyss,
Woodland beauty, a sweet remiss.

Beneath the boughs, a soft breeze sighs,
Painting the sky with its tender lies.
In this golden glow, our spirit flies,
A tapestry woven with whispered cries.

Rustling whispers, secrets long kept,
In the embrace of trees, we adept.
Golden hues where our hearts have leapt,
In this woodland dream, love is swept.

As twilight gathers, shadows expand,
Nature's wonders at our command.
Golden hues in a tender land,
A woodland reverie, close at hand.

Sparkling Hearth of the Woodland

In the heart of the woods, a fire glows bright,
Whispers of the leaves dance in the night.
Shadows flicker, stories unfold,
The warmth of the hearth, a tale retold.

Creatures draw close, in the softening light,
Murmurs and laughter, a joyous sight.
The spark of the fire, alive with glee,
Holds the secrets of nature, wild and free.

Embers drift gently, like stars in the air,
Illuminating dreams with a tender glare.
Beneath the tall oaks, under moon's embrace,
Harmony reigns in this sacred place.

Branches sway softly, a lullaby's tune,
Crickets are singing, beneath the moon.
Hope flickers on, like the flame in the night,
In the woodland's hearth, everything's right.

So gather 'round, let the stories flow,
The sparkling hearth, where hearts will grow.
In unity's glow, let the spirits rise,
In this woodland haven, 'neath infinite skies.

Brilliance Wrapped in Green

In the embrace of lush, verdant dreams,
Nature weaves magic, or so it seems.
Leaves whisper secrets in the morning light,
A tapestry woven, brilliant and bright.

Paths entwine under canopies grand,
Where flowers bloom, colorful and unplanned.
Golden rays filter through branches above,
Painting the world with nature's pure love.

In shadows deep, life dances and hums,
Bees buzz softly, while the sweet nectar comes.
Birds take to flight with melodious cheer,
In the brilliance of green, all is sincere.

With every step, the heart starts to race,
Finding the beauty in each tiny space.
The love of the wild, a sacred embrace,
In this blossomed haven, we find our place.

As the sun dips low, a golden refrain,
The brilliance wrapped in green will remain.
Forever we cherish this vibrant scene,
In nature's wonder, our spirits glean.

Starlit Silence of the Forest

Under the cloak of a velvet night,
The forest awakens, a wondrous sight.
Stars twinkle gently, like fireflies' glow,
In starlit silence, the mysteries flow.

Moonbeams cascade through the whispering trees,
Kissing the ground with a delicate breeze.
Owls softly hoot, a call from afar,
In this tranquil haven, we dream and star.

Footsteps are muted on the soft forest floor,
Nature's own chorus opens its door.
Crickets are singing, their melody sweet,
As night weaves a blanket, cozy and neat.

Each shadow holds stories of days gone by,
As whispers of breezes float softly and sigh.
The heart finds solace in night's soft embrace,
In the starlit silence, we find our place.

So let us wander, lost in the night,
Where starlit silence brings pure delight.
In the arms of the woods, we learn to believe,
In the magic and peace that the night can weave.

The Enchanted Grove Awaits

Beyond the thicket, where the wildflowers sway,
The enchanted grove calls, come join the play.
Whispering breezes carry sweet scents,
In this magical realm, where wonder is dense.

Moss carpets the ground, a cushion of green,
Where sunlight and shadow create a serene.
The ancient trees stand guard at the gate,
In their watchful embrace, we sit and await.

Ferns unfurl secrets, like scrolls of the past,
In this sacred space, time flows slowly, vast.
The brook sings a lullaby, soft and pure,
In the enchanted grove, our hearts find allure.

With every heartbeat, the magic expands,
Gathering wonder with nature's own hands.
Leaves rustle softly, a melody sweet,
Inviting our souls to dance and to greet.

So linger with me, in this grove so bright,
Where dreams take flight in the still of the night.
The enchanted grove waits, just for you,
With wonders untold and skies always blue.

The Dance of Light and Leaf

In whispers soft the branches swayed,
As sunlight filtered through the shade.
A dance of light, a play so bright,
Each leaf a spark, a fleeting sight.

The breeze would hum a gentle tune,
While shadows moved beneath the moon.
A tapestry of green and gold,
Each secret of the grove retold.

The sun would rise with warming grace,
Caressing every hidden place.
With laughter stitched in every beam,
Creating nature's radiant dream.

As evening draped its velvet cloak,
The trees conferred, and spirits spoke.
In twilight's glow, they danced anew,
Embracing night with a softer hue.

The dance continues, time will show,
As light and leaf in harmony grow.
A rhythm born of earth and sky,
Where moments linger, then drift by.

Ephemeral Gleams of Nature's Heart

Among the blooms, the light would play,
In colors bright, it weaves its way.
Each petal shines with dew-kissed dreams,
Ephemeral glints, like whispered beams.

The ancient trees stand tall and wise,
With stories cradled in their sighs.
Gleams of hope in every tear,
Nature's heart beats softly here.

The brook reflects the fleeting sun,
A melody where all is one.
With every ripple, every glance,
A moment caught in nature's dance.

As twilight draws the colors in,
The world prepares where dreams begin.
With stars appearing, hearts alight,
In silence shared, we find our night.

Ephemeral gleams, the finest art,
Forever dancing in nature's heart.
Held in time, then lost to air,
A fleeting glimpse, a gentle prayer.

Shiny Offerings Beneath the Canopy

Beneath the canopy so grand,
Shiny treasures grace the land.
Each glimmer tells a tale untold,
In colors bright and shades of gold.

The forest floor adorned with gems,
Nature's art, its diadems.
A sparkling array of life unfurled,
Each moment rich in this wild world.

With every step, a crunch below,
The leaves like whispers start to glow.
A dance of shadows, light will weave,
In quiet wonders, we believe.

The morning dew, a crystal gift,
In sunlight's arms, it starts to lift.
Each droplet sings of sweet delight,
Reflections pure, a shared invite.

The beauty rests in simple things,
As nature hums and gently sings.
Shiny offerings, gifts of grace,
Beneath the canopy's warm embrace.

Harmony of the Illuminated Grove

In the grove where shadows blend,
A harmony that none can end.
With rustling leaves and whispers low,
The heart of nature starts to glow.

Each branch, each bough, a note to play,
As light and dark both find their way.
In unity, they intertwine,
Creating magic, pure and fine.

The golden rays that cut the night,
Illuminate the world with light.
A symphony of breath and pause,
In every beat, the world because.

With creatures small and gentle grace,
The grove becomes a sacred place.
Where every whisper speaks of peace,
And in the stillness, worries cease.

Harmony of tree and ground,
In reverence, we gather round.
Illuminated paths might stray,
But in this grove, we choose to stay.

Sprightliness in Sylvan Light

In the woods where shadows play,
Gentle whispers greet the day.
Birds like notes in sweet refrain,
Echo through the leafy lane.

Sunbeams flicker, bright and gold,
Tales of magic yet untold.
Dancing leaves in breezy flight,
Sprightliness in sylvan light.

Where the streams begin to sing,
Life awakens, joy takes wing.
Nature's laughter fills the air,
In this vibrant, blissful lair.

Moss-clad stones and petals rare,
Softly cradle moments there.
Each step melds with earth and sky,
As we wander, hearts held high.

In the glade where dreams do meet,
Time stands still beneath our feet.
Every heartbeat knows delight,
In this realm of purest light.

Elysian Reflections on Forest Floors

Amid the boughs where breezes sigh,
Moss carpets like a prayer draped nigh.
Reflections shimmer, softly sound,
In this tranquil, sacred ground.

Petals dance on river's edge,
Whispers float on nature's pledge.
Every leaf a silent tale,
Elysian secrets in the vale.

Sunset paints the tree-kissed skies,
Amber hues where wonder lies.
Golden rays through branches break,
A tapestry that dreams awake.

Underneath the arching trees,
Time flows gently with the breeze.
Shadows weave their mystic art,
Bringing calm to every heart.

In the quiet, thoughts take flight,
Elysian visions come to light.
Endless peace on forest floors,
Nature's beauty ever soars.

Dance of the Sun Through Green Canopies

Through the leaves the sunlight spills,
Casting warmth on verdant hills.
A dance of rays in playful sway,
Guiding footsteps on our way.

Branches stretch, a vibrant sea,
Whispers soft, cocooned and free.
Nature beckons, come and see,
Life's embrace, our melody.

Each beam of light a fleeting kiss,
Lost in wonder, moments bliss.
Bright against the emerald hue,
Sunlight dances, pure and true.

In this chorus, shadows blend,
Every corner holds a friend.
Timeless beauty speaks in sighs,
As the sun begins to rise.

Every rustling leaf, a clue,
Of the joy that dwells in you.
So come and share this magic time,
In nature's rhythm, pure and prime.

The Shimmer of Secrets Held High

In twilight's glow, the world awakes,
Mysteries glow as daylight breaks.
Whispers of ages swept away,
In the evening's soft display.

Glimmers dance on water's face,
Secrets shimmer, leave no trace.
Stars emerge, their stories told,
In this fabric, rich and bold.

Dreams entwined with silken night,
Guided by the silver light.
Each shadow holds a hidden spark,
As we wander through the dark.

Hearts entwined with hope's delight,
Embrace the magic, hold it tight.
In the stillness, truth concedes,
Secret gardens, timeless deeds.

So let the night unveil the skies,
With every twinkle, truths arise.
In the quiet, we shall find,
The shimmer of secrets held in mind.

Whispers of the Evergreen

In the forest, secrets dwell,
Between the trees, a gentle spell.
Leaves rustle softly, tales unfold,
Whispers of life, both new and old.

Sunlight dapples on the ground,
Nature's heartbeat, a soothing sound.
Moss carpets, lush and bright green,
A sanctuary, so serene.

Birds sing high, a joyful cheer,
Echoing whispers, drawing near.
Branches sway in the warm embrace,
An enchanted, timeless space.

Through tangled roots, dreams will grow,
In this haven, time moves slow.
Under boughs where shadows play,
Peaceful echoes lead the way.

As dusk descends, the stars ignite,
In the woods, all feels just right.
Whispers of the evergreen sing,
Nature's magic, a sacred ring.

Shimmering Shadows Above

Underneath the moonlit sky,
Shadows shimmer, drifting high.
Stars blink gently, secrets shared,
In the night, all are ensnared.

Cool winds dance through the trees,
Carrying soft melodies.
Whispers float on air so sweet,
Guided by the heartbeat's beat.

Branches bow in silent grace,
Swaying slow, they find their place.
Moonlight trickles, silver beams,
Weaving through our quiet dreams.

The world beneath is hushed, still,
While shadows glow on the hill.
In this moment, hearts align,
In the glow, we feel divine.

As dawn approaches, colors bloom,
Shadows dance, dispelling gloom.
Beneath the sky, a brand new start,
In shimmering light, we find our heart.

Under the Canopy of Dreams

Beneath branches, woven tight,
Dreams emerge in soft twilight.
Whispers echo, softly sway,
Guiding hopes along the way.

Leaves embrace each cherished thought,
Where the heart and soul are sought.
Fleeting moments, gently cast,
Under the canopy, dreams hold fast.

Dreamers gather, stories shared,
In this space, we feel cared.
Laughter dances through the air,
Creating magic, a bond rare.

As nightfall drapes, the stars align,
In dreams' embrace, worlds combine.
Nature's whisper, soft and low,
Guides us where we wish to go.

In this haven, we find our way,
Carving paths where spirits play.
Underneath the emerald arch,
In the woods, we make our march.

Celestial Needles Sway

Pines rise tall, in grace they sway,
Underneath the skies of gray.
Celestial needles whisper deep,
In the forest, secrets keep.

Mountains cradle the fading light,
Stars awaken, slipping bright.
Gentle breezes brush our cheeks,
Nature's language softly speaks.

Waves of green in earthy hues,
Echoes of the morning dews.
Under twilight, shadows merge,
Within the stillness, dreams emerge.

Each needle holds a story told,
Of quiet strength and boughs of gold.
In these woods, our spirits play,
Forever changed by nature's way.

As the mist begins to rise,
We seek solace in the skies.
Celestial needles guide us there,
In the forest, we breathe prayer.

Enchanted Spirits in Twilight Shadows

In the hush of evening light,
Whispers break through twilight's veil.
Shadows dance, a ghostly sight,
Softly told in ancient tale.

Flickering dreams on fading beams,
Twining through the forest's heart.
Silhouettes weave silvery seams,
Where silence plays a mystic part.

Stars peer down with eager eyes,
As the moon unveils her grace.
In this realm where magic lies,
Spirits twirl in free embrace.

Echoes of a bygone song,
Guide the wanderers that roam.
In the dark where shadows throng,
Enchanted night calls us home.

So we linger, hearts aligned,
With the whispers soft and low.
In the twilight, fate entwined,
Among the spirits' gentle flow.

The Dance of the Light-Dripped Woods

Golden rays through canopies,
Dancing gently with the breeze.
Leaves are swaying, swirls with ease,
Nature's rhythm, sweet and free.

Mossy carpets cradle feet,
As the sun begins to fade.
In this grove, life feels complete,
Each moment, pure and unmade.

Branches stretch with whispered grace,
Coaxing secrets from the ground.
Here, the heart finds its own pace,
In the woods where dreams are found.

Laughter echoes, shadows play,
Nature's choir singing bright.
All who wander lose their way,
In this dance of pure delight.

Every step a timeless waltz,
Silent stories interlace.
In the woods, no faults or faults,
Just the joy of nature's embrace.

Whispers Illuminated by Leaves

Underneath the leafy dome,
Softly secrets start to weave.
Nature's breath begins to roam,
In the quiet, souls believe.

Luminous beams filter through,
Painting whispers on the ground.
In this world of vibrant hue,
Every heartbeat echoes sound.

Branches sway with gentle might,
Holding stories they have known.
Every rustle, pure delight,
In a language all its own.

Winds that carry ancient lore,
Hug the trunks with tender touch.
Every moment asks for more,
In the wild, we crave so much.

Glimmers of sunlight's embrace,
Spark the leaves to life anew.
In this sacred, quiet space,
Whispers transform into true.

Mirth of the Forest in Radiant Glare

Amidst the trees, the laughter rings,
Echoes through the vibrant air.
Nature sings of all her things,
Joyful moments everywhere.

With the blush of dawn's first light,
Sunbeams glisten on each face.
Creatures dart, a living sight,
In this wilderness of grace.

Petals dance in sunlight's glow,
While the brook hums its sweet tune.
In the forest, time moves slow,
Bathed in colors of the noon.

Every leaf a silent cheer,
In the warmth of golden rays.
In this splendor, hearts draw near,
Lost within these magical days.

So we twirl in bright delight,
Embraced by the vibrant air.
In the forest's purest light,
Mirth and wonder, everywhere.

Subtle Radiance of Leafy Giants

In emerald whispers, leaves reside,
Where shadows play and secrets hide.
Among tall trunks, they sway and dance,
Inviting dreams in a delicate trance.

Beneath the branches, sunlight gleams,
Nature's beauty weaves our dreams.
With gentle breezes, life takes flight,
In this embrace, we're held so tight.

A tapestry of green unfolds,
Each leaf tells tales that nature holds.
From ancient roots to tips so high,
In leafy giants, we find the sky.

The air is fresh, the heart is free,
Amongst the giants, I'm meant to be.
With every breath, I come alive,
In their presence, my spirit thrives.

The subtle radiance softly glows,
In every corner, the magic flows.
Within nature's arms, we find our place,
In leafy giants, a sacred space.

Enchanted Solitudes of the Thicket

In thickets dense, where whispers dwell,
The heart finds peace, a tranquil spell.
Amongst the shadows, secrets bloom,
In nature's cradle, we find room.

A songbird's call breaks the still air,
In enchanted solitudes, we share.
The rustle of leaves, soft and sweet,
In hidden paths, our spirits meet.

Mossy beds hold a gentle hope,
In the thicket's arms, we learn to cope.
Branches intertwine, a sacred thread,
In each moment, new life is spread.

Ferns unfurl in shades of green,
In this haven, peace is seen.
With every step, the world retreats,
In the thicket's heart, my spirit beats.

The sun filters through, a golden glance,
Guiding souls in nature's dance.
In enchanted solitudes, we roam,
Finding in stillness, a sense of home.

The Gleam of Life in the Canopy

In the canopy's embrace, life ignites,
Sunbeams filter through soaring heights.
Leaves shimmer like jewels on high,
In their glow, we glimpse the sky.

Birds take flight, with wings spread wide,
Chasing dreams and the thrill of the ride.
Amongst the branches, life intertwines,
In this realm, the spirit aligns.

Swaying gently, the branches sing,
Of ancient stories and vibrant spring.
Every rustle holds a tale,
In the forest's heart, we shall prevail.

The gleam of life shines all around,
With every heartbeat, magic is found.
In the canopy, dreams take form,
A refuge dear, a sacred storm.

Through leaves and light, our souls ascend,
In the forest's arms, we find a friend.
The whispers of nature fill the air,
In the canopy's glow, we learn to care.

Nature's Jewels Among the Roots

Beneath the earth, where shadows creep,
Nature's jewels lie hidden deep.
Roots intertwine in silent grace,
In this dark haven, life finds its place.

Mushrooms bloom, a fragrant sight,
Amongst the roots in dim twilight.
With every whisper, the soil breathes,
In sacred grounds, the heart believes.

The gentle touch of the morning dew,
Awakens life, fresh and new.
Among the roots, stories unfold,
Of ages past, of dreams retold.

In nature's realm, we seek the truth,
Among the roots, we find our youth.
With every step, a treasure found,
In quiet mysteries, we are bound.

Nature's jewels spark and gleam,
In the soil lies a tranquil dream.
Among the roots, our spirits soar,
In this embrace, we crave for more.

Frosted Feathers in the Sky

Soft whispers drift through wide blue,
Feathers kissed by morning dew.
Clouds like blankets, pure and white,
Hiding dreams out of our sight.

A chilly breeze, a gentle sigh,
Dances through the winter sky.
Nature's breath on frosted wings,
In silence, beauty softly sings.

Silhouettes of trees appear,
Frozen branches, stark and clear.
The world adorned in icy grace,
A moment held in time and space.

Beneath the vast and open dome,
Birds begin their journey home.
With every flap, they break the hush,
As day awakes in vibrant rush.

And in the glow of morning light,
The frosted feathers take their flight.
Through the chill, their spirits soar,
In the sky, forevermore.

Illuminated by Nature's Touch

The sun spills gold on petals bright,
Painting gardens pure with light.
Flowers sway as breezes play,
A symphony of bright array.

Shadows dance beneath each tree,
Nature whispers, wild and free.
Each leaf glows with vibrant hue,
Revealing secrets fresh and new.

Birds carve arcs against the blue,
Songs of joy in morning's dew.
The brook laughs as it finds its way,
A shimmering path where children play.

Mountains rise, their peaks aglow,
With sparkling crowns of melting snow.
Rays of warmth, a gentle caress,
Bring forth a world in sweet finesse.

To breathe the air, both sweet and clear,
To roam where nature holds us dear.
Illumined by love, we feel the touch,
Of life entwined, we owe so much.

The Luminous Forest Breathes

In the heart where shadows blend,
The forest whispers, secrets send.
Leaves shimmer with a silvery sheen,
A tranquil space, peaceful and serene.

Branches weave a cozy nest,
Where spirits linger, feel the rest.
Moss carpets ground with velvet soft,
In this embrace, our hearts take off.

Moonlight drapes a silver shroud,
The night enfolds us like a crowd.
Crickets sing a lullaby tune,
As stars unveil their glowing boon.

Each step taken feels profound,
In the silence, magic found.
The trees stand tall, guardians wise,
Their stories echo through the skies.

As dawn approaches, colors wake,
The luminous forest begins to shake.
Gentle breaths of life unfold,
As new tales of wonder are told.

Sylvan Secrets at Dawn

Morning light begins to creep,
Through the branches, dreams we keep.
In the stillness, shadows flee,
Revealing treasures wild and free.

Mist hovers like whispered prayer,
Nature's secrets fill the air.
Each petal glistens, dew adorned,
With promises of life reborn.

Birds unfurl their wings in flight,
Chasing echoes of the night.
A chorus rises, fresh and sweet,
In the realm where daylight meets.

Footsteps soft upon the trail,
Each sound tells a vibrant tale.
In the tapestry of green,
A convergence of the seen and unseen.

Sylvan whispers, soft and low,
In the dawn, our spirits grow.
With every breath, we find our place,
In nature's warm and sweet embrace.

Shimmering Shadows Beneath the Firs

Beneath the firs, the shadows play,
Whispers of night, stealing the day.
Leaves flutter soft in the gentle breeze,
Secrets are kept among the trees.

Moonlight dances on velvety ground,
In silence, the mystery is profound.
Stars twinkle bright in an inky sky,
While dreams of the forest slowly sigh.

Footsteps echo through the quiet night,
Guided by the soft, glowing light.
The world outside fades, it's just us here,
Embraced by shadows we hold so dear.

A breeze carries stories of old,
Whispers of magic waiting to unfold.
With every rustle, the night draws near,
In shimmering shadows, nothing to fear.

Together we'll wander until the dawn,
Through shimmering secrets night has drawn.
As daylight creeps in, we'll bid farewell,
To shimmering shadows, we know so well.

Reverie in a Sunlit Glade

In a sunlit glade, where wildflowers bloom,
Radiant warmth dispels the gloom.
Birds sing sweetly, a gentle refrain,
Nature's chorus will never wane.

Butterflies flutter, a delicate dance,
In this tranquil place, lost in a trance.
Golden rays filter through the trees,
Embracing the glade with a gentle breeze.

With every step, the heart starts to soar,
In this paradise, we long for more.
Branches weave tales of moments divine,
As sunlight drips like honeyed wine.

Laughter resounds, earthy and free,
Among the flowers, just you and me.
Days like these are jewels of time,
A symphony of beauty, a perfect rhyme.

As shadows elongate, day's respite,
We cherish the glade bathed in light.
In our reverie, memories will stay,
Forever entwined in sun's warm sway.

Dewdrop Serenade on Branches

In morning's hush, the world awakes,
Dewdrops glisten, the heart it takes.
Each tiny sphere, a world in itself,
Hanging like jewels on nature's shelf.

Whispers of dawn weave through the leaves,
Sings a serenade, the spirit receives.
With every glimmer, dreams take flight,
In the delicate dance of morning light.

Branches cradle the weight of the morn,
Softly adorned, each silver adorn.
Nature's embrace, so tender and kind,
In the quiet spaces, peace we find.

As sunlight rises, the dew starts to fade,
A fleeting glimpse of the magic made.
But in our hearts, the serenade lingers,
Like whispered secrets from nature's fingers.

So let us wander where the dewdrops lie,
And listen closely as the moments fly.
In the embrace of branches, dreams will grow,
In the dewdrop serenade, love's sweet glow.

Twilight Revelations Among the Trees

In twilight's glow, a veil hangs low,
The forest breathes, with secrets to show.
Shadows stretch long, whispering truths,
Revelations found in the heart of youth.

A rustle of leaves, a call from the night,
Stars begin to twinkle, a softening light.
Crisp air carries tales of old,
Among the trees, mysteries unfold.

Footfalls echo through path's embrace,
Familiar faces in nature's grace.
With every heartbeat, the magic ignites,
In twilight's realm, the world unites.

Fingers brushing against the bark,
In every shadow, a glimmering spark.
Wisdom of ages, held in the leaves,
Twilight whispers, and the heart believes.

As night blankets the world with its shroud,
Among the trees, we stand unbowed.
In twilight revelations, we find our way,
With nature's embrace, we'll forever stay.

Luminescent Slopes of Serenity

In the hush of dawn's embrace,
Whispers dance on the soft grass.
Color blooms in every place,
Nature's beauty will surpass.

Gentle breezes brush the trees,
A symphony so sweetly played.
Serenity flows with ease,
In this tranquil, sunlit glade.

Mountains wear a golden crown,
As the day begins to rise.
Shadows stretch and softly drown,
Beneath the vast and open skies.

Clouds drift lazily above,
Painting dreams in the blue.
Every moment whispers love,
In a world both fresh and new.

Footsteps echo on the trail,
Where silence sings its soft song.
In this wonder, we can't fail,
Together we will roam along.

Dance of the Sunlit Conifers

Amidst the trees, the light will play,
Softly weaving shadows long.
Branches sway in bright ballet,
Nature hums a gentle song.

Golden rays through needles shine,
As the forest comes alive.
Every heartbeat feels divine,
In this place, the spirits thrive.

Whispers carry on the breeze,
Echoing the joy we share.
Dancing leaves with graceful ease,
Filling hearts with forest air.

Sunlit paths invite our feet,
Guiding dreams with every step.
In this magic, life feels sweet,
Tangled roots where secrets kept.

Nature laughs in the bright light,
Holding wonders, soft and clear.
With each moment, pure delight,
In the woods, we shed our fear.

Celestial Lullabies in the Woodlands

Stars twinkle through the emerald leaves,
Moonlight kisses the whispering vines.
Nature sings as the magic weaves,
Softly cradling the night's designs.

Crickets chirp their soothing song,
As the world begins to dream.
In the stillness, we belong,
Lost in this celestial stream.

Echoes of laughter fill the air,
Fireflies dance in twilight's glow.
Caught in moments we share,
As the gentle night winds blow.

Trees like guardians stand tall,
Wrapped in stories yet untold.
In their embrace, we feel the thrall,
Of the mystery they hold.

Beneath the stars, our hearts take flight,
In the woodlands, dreams ignite.
Celestial lullabies, so bright,
Guide us through the deepening night.

A Glimmer Beneath the Canopy

In shadows deep, a glimmer glows,
Where the wildflowers gently sway.
Amidst the ferns, a secret knows,
The beauty of the trees at play.

Sunbeams filter, soft and warm,
Painting colors across the ground.
Every moment feels like charm,
In this magic, joy is found.

Mossy paths and winding streams,
Guide the wanderers at heart.
Tangled roots hold hidden dreams,
Where adventure finds its start.

Creatures stir in the gentle hush,
Life awakens with a sigh.
In the stillness, feel the rush,
Of the world breathing nearby.

Nestled under nature's dome,
Every heartbeat finds its rhyme.
In the woods, we feel at home,
Where the clock forgets its time.

Luminescence Through the Boughs

In twilight's glow, the branches sway,
Soft whispers weave through dusk's ballet.
Stars peek down with twinkling eyes,
Their silver beams the night supplies.

Leaves shimmer softly, a gentle dance,
Branches cradle dreams, a fleeting glance.
Moonlight spills on the forest floor,
Casting shadows, opening doors.

An owl hoots, a distant call,
Nature's symphony, entwined with all.
Echoes linger in the cool night air,
A serene moment, free from care.

With every step, the magic grows,
In quiet places, luminescence glows.
The heart beats fast, in tune with the night,
Guided by stars, pure and bright.

Echoes of Light on Soft Moss

Morning breaks with a gentle sigh,
Sunbeams dance as they flutter by.
Soft moss blankets the forest bed,
Holding whispers of dreams long spread.

In this haven, shadows play,
Laughter of sunlight, night fades away.
Each step a cradle of nature's grace,
In the warm embrace of this sacred space.

Raindrops glisten like jeweled tears,
Memories linger, vanquishing fears.
The earth breathes deep with every pulse,
A rhythm of life that none can repulse.

Footfalls light upon emerald green,
Echoes of light where the soul has been.
In every fiber, stories bloom,
A tapestry woven from nature's loom.

Resplendent Reflections of the Past

Mirrored waters catch the sky,
Where time stands still and whispers sigh.
In deep stillness, memories glow,
Reflecting tales of long ago.

Ancient trees, with stories entwined,
Guard the secrets of humankind.
Each wrinkle in bark, a chapter spun,
Echoes of laughter, of loss, of fun.

Upon the pond, the moonlight drapes,
An artist's brush in twilight shapes.
Rippling echoes of love long lost,
In every ripple, a tale embossed.

Resplendent dawn brings forth the day,
Yet shadows linger, do not stray.
Embrace the past, let memories last,
In the silent echoes, the die is cast.

Shining Beacons in the Wilderness

Upon the hill, the lantern glows,
A guiding light where the river flows.
In wild embrace, the night unfolds,
Stars ignite tales, countless and bold.

The wind carries whispers of old,
Stories of courage, of hearts turned cold.
Each flicker a promise, a path to tread,
In shadows of silence, destiny's thread.

Through tangled growth, the light will shine,
Illuminating dreams, both yours and mine.
Beneath the vastness, we take our stand,
As shining beacons in this wild land.

The call of the wild, a sweet refrain,
In the heart of the wilderness, we remain.
With every dawn, new hopes arise,
Beneath the tapestry of endless skies.

Frosted Fronds Under Starry Skies

Frosted fronds dance in the night,
Glittering cold, a wondrous sight.
Under stars, whispers freeze,
Nature's beauty, softly tease.

The moon weaves silver in the trees,
While winter's breath carries a breeze.
Each leaf glimmers with frozen grace,
In this stillness, find your place.

Night unfolds with celestial light,
In the dark, a serene delight.
Frosted fronds in quiet pose,
A world wrapped in silent prose.

Together they shimmer, twinkling bright,
Guided by the stars' soft might.
In the hush of night, we find,
A gentle peace, a calm of mind.

Beneath the silk of starry glow,
Silent whispers begin to flow.
Together, we can drift and sway,
In the frosted dreams of ballet.

Verdant Glow in the Morning Mist

Dew-kissed leaves in the sun's embrace,
Verdant glow, nature's grace.
Morning mist begins to rise,
Whispering secrets, soft and wise.

Sunlight dances on the grass,
Creating shadows as moments pass.
In this calm, the world awakes,
A serene beauty, a path it makes.

Birds sing sweetly in the trees,
Carried softly on the breeze.
Every note a joyful cheer,
Heralding a brand new year.

As the light pierces the fog,
Nature unveils her morning log.
Each moment holds a precious spark,
In the glow, we leave our mark.

Verdant fields stretch far and wide,
An endless canvas, love and pride.
In the mist's embrace, we remain,
Cherishing life's gentle refrain.

Enveloped in Nature's Diamond Veil

Morning dew like diamonds shine,
Nature's gift, a design divine.
Enveloped in a quiet cocoon,
Life awakens, oblivious tune.

Petals glisten in soft light,
Every color, a pure delight.
Nature's veil wraps around tight,
Cradling dreams into the night.

Whispers float on gentle air,
A lullaby of sweet despair.
In this haven, time stands still,
Heartbeats echo, soft and shrill.

Emerald leaves sway slowly low,
As if they feel the world below.
In the calm, we seek to find,
Peace encased, nature's kind.

Enveloped in this diamond glow,
Moments freeze, the world moves slow.
Held within this serene veil,
Life's true beauty will prevail.

Aura of Solitude in Tall Trunks

Tall trunks stand, a silent guard,
In their shade, the heart is scarred.
An aura of solitude calls me near,
Amidst the stillness, I quietly hear.

Bark rough against the tender hand,
Nature whispers across the land.
Each tree a story, each branch a sigh,
Beneath their watch, life reruns the sky.

In the forest, a sacred space,
Tranquil thoughts begin to trace.
An echo hidden deep within,
Solitude's song, a secret spin.

The canopy billows like a dream,
Filtering light with a gentle beam.
In the tall trunks' comforting shade,
Find solace where worries fade.

With every breath, I feel at home,
In whispers shared, I cease to roam.
The aura wraps like a warm caress,
In solitude, I find my rest.

Twilight's Embrace on Foliage

In whispers soft, the daylight fades,
A cloak of dusk on leafy glades.
Colors blend, a painter's dream,
Night's first kiss, a gentle beam.

Shadows dance on emerald hues,
Nature sighs with evening's cues.
Each rustling leaf, a story told,
In twilight's arms, the world unfolds.

The air turns cool, a sweet reprieve,
As stars awaken, softly weave.
Among the branches, secrets lay,
In twilight's embrace, stillness stays.

A chorus springs from hidden nooks,
The nightingale sings from shadowed crooks.
A symphony in the dark's embrace,
Underneath the moon's soft lace.

Foliage sways in harmony,
Boundless beauty, wild and free.
In twilight's touch, all spirits roam,
The forest breathes, it feels like home.

Spruce and Sparkle at Dusk

Spruce trees stand with pride alight,
Beneath the sky, a sapphire night.
Twinkling lights in every cone,
Nature's gems, so brightly shone.

Whispers of wind, a soft caress,
Boughs adorned in evening's dress.
Crickets chirp their lullabies,
As twilight paints the vast, wide skies.

Golden rays begin to fade,
In shadowed groves where dreams are made.
The sparkle fades, but magic stays,
In dusky realms that night displays.

Underneath the twilight's dome,
Spruce and sparkle truly roam.
Each branch a whisper, soft and pure,
A tranquil world, forever sure.

With every breath, the night unfolds,
In mystery, the heart beholds.
Spruce and sparkle, take your flight,
In dusk's embrace, in soft twilight.

The Hidden Radiance of the Woods

Amid the trees, a subtle glow,
Where sunlit beams through branches flow.
Colors dance with gentle grace,
In nature's heart, a sacred place.

Hidden wonders softly gleam,
In dappled light, the shadows dream.
Each footfall whispers tales untold,
In the woods of hidden gold.

Ferns unfurl in emerald hues,
Soft petals kissed by morning dew.
The air is thick with sweet perfume,
A gentle sigh, all fears consume.

With every breath, the magic stirs,
Awakening the heart that purrs.
The hidden radiance, pure and bright,
Illuminates the veil of night.

In quiet corners, secrets lie,
Beneath the vast and starry sky.
Bound by roots, yet free like birds,
In the woods, we find our words.

Moonlit Sentinels of Nature

In the night's embrace, they stand tall,
Moonlit sentinels, proud to call.
Protectors of dreams, of lore untold,
In silver light, their stories unfold.

Branches arch like arms embraced,
In night's soft glow, all fear is chased.
Secrets whispered on the breeze,
With every rustle, hearts find ease.

The moon, a lantern in the sky,
Watches over with a watchful eye.
Each shadow cast, a tale relayed,
In nature's theater, fears allayed.

By the stream's edge, reflections gleam,
Twinkling stars, in a cosmic dream.
Moonlit sentinels of nature guide,
In tranquil moments, love abides.

All creatures pause, a spellbound trance,
In silver light, we share a dance.
Under the watchful, starlit skies,
Nature's beauty, where magic lies.

Silver Threads Among the Boughs

In twilight's glow, the branches sway,
With silver threads that dance and play.
They shimmer softly, whisper low,
Beneath the stars, where secrets flow.

The moonlight weaves a silken path,
While shadows cast a gentle wrath.
Each glimmer tells of nights long past,
Where memories linger, unsurpassed.

Among the leaves, the stories weave,
Of dreams once chased, of hopes believed.
In every thread, a tale unfolds,
Of silver charms and joys retold.

The breeze carries the echoes sweet,
As branches bend and hearts do meet.
In nature's quilt, we find our peace,
Where silver threads will never cease.

So let us pause, in wonder stand,
And trace the threads with gentle hand.
For in the boughs, our spirits soar,
Where silver threads unite us more.

Echoes of the Forest Canopy

In the forest's heart, a whisper grows,
Echoes of life, where the wild wind blows.
Each rustle and murmur, a secret shared,
A canopy's song, lovingly bared.

Leaves join in chorus, a dance so light,
As shadows play in the fading light.
Branches embrace, the sky they kiss,
In this sacred space, a tranquil bliss.

The call of the owl, a haunting tune,
A serenade beneath the moon.
While crickets and frogs join in the night,
Their symphony weaves a world of delight.

Each step through the woods, a path to take,
Where echoes linger, and dreams awake.
In the embrace of the whispering trees,
We find our refuge, our soul's release.

From dawn to dusk, the kingdom thrives,
In echoes of love, the forest survives.
With every sigh, every gentle sway,
The spirit of nature guides our way.

Radiant Needles in the Wind

The pines stand tall, their needles gleam,
In sunlight's embrace, they catch a dream.
Each radiant hue, a story bright,
A tapestry woven in nature's light.

With whispers low, the branches sigh,
As breezes dance and spirits fly.
In rustling leaves, a melody plays,
Guiding our hearts through golden rays.

The world beneath is calm and still,
As nature's echoes our senses fill.
In needles sharp, the beauty lies,
Reflecting wisdom from ancient skies.

In twilight's glow, the pines will stand,
Their needles bright, a guiding hand.
Through storms and trials, they'll endure,
A testament of strength, steadfast and pure.

So when the winds begin to stir,
Remember the joy that nature's blur.
In radiant needles, find your peace,
As the whispering pines offer their lease.

The Enchanted Grove of Glitter

In the heart of the woods, a grove so rare,
Where sunlight dances in the air.
With glittering leaves that catch the light,
A magical realm, pure delight.

The flowers bloom in colors bright,
A wondrous show, a painter's sight.
Each petal holds a tale, a dream,
In this enchanted realm, we gleam.

The brook nearby sings a gentle song,
A symphony sweet, where we belong.
Its waters shimmer as they flow,
Through the grove where secrets grow.

With every step, the magic breathes,
In whispers soft, the forest weaves.
Inviting souls to linger near,
To cherish joy, to conquer fear.

Among the trees, the spirits glide,
In swirling forms, they laugh and bide.
In the enchanted grove of glitter bright,
We'll find our dreams and endless light.

Radiance Among the Branches

In the stillness of the eve,
Sunlight dapples on the leaves,
Golden hues of warming light,
Whispers dance in gentle flight.

Breezes weave through trees so tall,
Nature's breath, a soothing call,
Petals drift like thoughts untold,
In this magic, hearts unfold.

Colors blend in sweet embrace,
Radiance finds its rightful place,
Every branch a story shared,
In the light, all souls are bared.

Underneath the leafy crown,
Peaceful thoughts do not drown,
Embers glow as shadows play,
Time is still, here we stay.

A moment's grace, the world slows down,
In this haven, love's renown,
Hearts connected, spirits rise,
Radiance seen through open eyes.

Twinkling Secrets of the Woods

Among the trees, the secrets lie,
Whispers carried through the sky,
Twinkling stars in twilight's breath,
Stories of the woods, in depth.

Each path winds with a hidden scene,
Mossy stones where dreams have been,
Crickets sing and leaves respond,
Nature's lullaby, a fond.

Shadows stretch as night descends,
Magic flows, the heart transcends,
Fireflies light the dusky air,
Revealing truths that few may dare.

In this place, the wild is free,
Boughs that hold the mystery,
Every rustle holds a tale,
On the breeze, the voices sail.

Through the dark, we wander near,
Twinkling secrets, bright and clear,
In this realm of whispered sounds,
Harmony and peace abounds.

Glimmering Treetops Beneath the Moon

Under the watch of silver light,
Treetops shimmer, pure delight,
Moonbeams dance on leaves so bright,
Guiding dreams through endless night.

The whisper of the evening breeze,
Carries tales from ancient trees,
Glimmers speak in light's embrace,
In this haven, we find grace.

Branches sway in soft surrender,
Cradling hopes, their sweetest tender,
Each twinkle holds a silent vow,
In the moment, here and now.

Stars reflect in calmest streams,
Nature stirs our wildest dreams,
Glimmering light where shadows blend,
A canvas where our souls ascend.

Wrapped in night, we feel alive,
Beneath the moon, our spirits thrive,
In this glimmer, all is bright,
A world transformed by gentle light.

Dappled Light and Nature's Song

Among the trees, a soft refrain,
Dappled light, a sweet campaign,
Nature's song in every hue,
Calls the heart to start anew.

Birds take flight on whispers sweet,
In the branches, melodies meet,
Leaves applaud with gentle sway,
Marking every joyful play.

Sunbeams filter through the green,
Creating moments rarely seen,
Each note flows on the breeze,
Carrying with it, our ease.

The rustling leaves compose a tune,
Echoing beneath the moon,
On this path, our spirits dance,
In nature's grasp, an endless chance.

With every step, our hearts unite,
In the dappled, soft twilight,
Celebrating life and song,
In this beauty, we belong.

A Harmony Woven with Light

Morning breaks with golden hues,
Birds sing softly in the dew.
Whispers dance upon the breeze,
Nature's symphony aims to please.

Shimmering rays through leaves do play,
Inviting every heart to sway.
A canvas bright, a melody,
Together, we find harmony.

Each petal glows in gentle grace,
Sunlight paints love on each face.
In laughter shared, in silence deep,
In this warm embrace, we leap.

Clouds drift slowly, soft and light,
In their shadows, dreams take flight.
Boundless skies, a world in view,
In every hue, life feels anew.

Together we weave through day and night,
In every moment, pure delight.
With hands entwined, we journey far,
A harmony woven, beneath the stars.

Sculpted Peace of the Granitic Realm

Mountains rise with ancient grace,
Silent giants in their place.
Granite stands through time and tide,
A deep-rooted, steadfast guide.

Underneath the moon's soft gaze,
Whispers echo through the haze.
Calm flows through each rocky seam,
Nature's peace, a shared dream.

Mossy stones in shadows hide,
Where gentle streams and songbirds chide.
Each step taken on this ground,
A tranquil heart will surely be found.

In twilight's blush, the world sleeps tight,
Stars awaken, glowing bright.
In the stillness, spirits meet,
In this place, our souls feel complete.

Sculpted by time, the mountains stand,
Guardians of this sacred land.
With every breath, we seek to feel,
The peace within this granitic seal.

Shards of Color in Nature's Canopy

Beneath the boughs, a tapestry,
Colors splash so wild and free.
Sunlight filters, diamonds fall,
Nature's bounty enchants us all.

Leaves of emerald, flowers bright,
Bring the canvas to pure light.
Rustling laughter of the trees,
Whispers dance upon the breeze.

A rainbow's edge in morning dew,
Reflections of a world so true.
Petals flutter, shadows play,
In every moment, time holds sway.

With every glance, a story's told,
Nature's palette, bright and bold.
In this beauty, hearts ignite,
Shards of color, pure delight.

As night approaches, colors fade,
But dreams of daylight are relayed.
In nature's arms, we find our way,
Forever caught in vibrant sway.

The Luster of Wilderness Unveiled

Hidden trails weave through the trees,
In the stillness, one can breathe.
Wilderness calls with a gentle hand,
Inviting us to this wild land.

Moonlit nights and sunlit days,
Nature's tune in numerous ways.
The luster shines in untamed grace,
In every shadow, a sacred space.

Footfalls soft on forest floor,
Every echo, a whispered lore.
Mountains stand in quiet proud,
Veils of mist, nature's shroud.

Creatures roam in search of peace,
In their presence, worries cease.
The wild heart beats loud and free,
In every rustle, we hear the key.

The luster of this world unfolds,
With stories whispered, dreams retold.
In the wild, we find our soul,
A sense of belonging makes us whole.

Flickering Dreams Between Stems

In the meadow's gentle sway,
Whispers dance on twilight's breath,
Every shadow tells a tale,
Softly weaving dreams of depth.

Petals glisten with a hue,
Caught in starlight's tender gleam,
Hopes suspended in the dew,
Fleeting like a fragile dream.

Dancing leaves in softest flight,
Catch the sighs of whispered breaths,
Every moment feels so right,
Life unfolds in fleeting threads.

Beneath the moon's enchanting gaze,
Night unveils its gentle charms,
Every flicker serenades,
Lulling hearts within its arms.

Flickering dreams embraced in light,
Cradle whispers of the night,
In the garden, spirits soar,
Bound in love forevermore.

The Flicker Beneath the Needles

Beneath the needles, shadows play,
Sparkling lights in colors deep,
Nature's secrets drift and sway,
In the stillness, spirits leap.

Sunbeams dapple on the ground,
Painting stories with each glint,
Every heartbeat makes a sound,
In the forest's quiet hint.

Rustling leaves, a gentle song,
Echoes through the ancient trees,
Where the lost and found belong,
Whispered truths ride on the breeze.

While the shadows flicker near,
Embers glow in twilight's calm,
Every flicker brings us near,
Cradled in the evening's balm.

The flicker beneath the needles,
Weaves a tapestry of light,
In the heart, a gentle seed will,
Spark the dreams that feel just right.

Suspended Moments in Woodland Glow

In the woodland, magic stirs,
Suspended moments in the air,
Glowing softly as it purrs,
Nature's breath a whispered prayer.

Every branch tells tales untold,
Glimmers caught in twilight's hand,
Memories wrapped in amber gold,
Dancing softly, they will stand.

Beneath the veil of evening's shade,
Quiet thoughts begin to bloom,
Every corner of the glade,
Holds a hint of night's perfume.

Crickets sing their lullabies,
Notes suspended on the breeze,
Through the trees, the starry skies,
Gather dreams like autumn leaves.

Suspended moments wrapped in glow,
Silent wonders intertwine,
In the heart of woods, we sow,
Seeds of dreams that brightly shine.

Prism of Shadows Among the Pines

Among the pines, a prism shines,
Shadows weave in dusk's embrace,
Life unfolds in whispered lines,
Every breath, a brief trace.

Pathways carved with gentle care,
Twilight spills its golden hue,
Flickers dance upon the air,
Telling tales both old and new.

In the calm, the heart takes flight,
Fluttering like a wayward dream,
Captured in the waning light,
Life's reflections softly gleam.

Branches cradle night's repose,
Stars emerge with ancient glow,
In the stillness, magic flows,
Echoing what we may know.

Prism of shadows, softly cast,
Secrets held in nature's art,
Every moment, shadows past,
Whisper stories to the heart.

Veils of Light in the Timber

In the forest's quiet embrace,
Sunlight dances, leaves interlace.
Shadows whisper through the trees,
Nature's secrets on the breeze.

Golden rays pierce through the mist,
Every moment feels like bliss.
A tapestry of green and gold,
Stories of the wild unfold.

Footfalls softened by the earth,
Each step echoes nature's birth.
Veils of light in tranquil glades,
Where peace and magic never fades.

Branches sway in gentle tune,
Underneath the watchful moon.
A symphony of rustling leaves,
Nature's heart that never grieves.

In the depths of ancient trees,
Whispers float upon the breeze.
Veils of light, a fleeting dream,
Nature's canvas, pure and serene.

The Magical Shimmer of Earth's Guardians

Among the rocks and vibrant blooms,
Life awakens, dispels glooms.
Nature's guardians, strong and wise,
Hidden magic beneath the skies.

Crystals spark in morning's glow,
Whispers of the earth below.
Each leaf glistens, life takes flight,
A treasure trove of pure delight.

In every stream where waters flow,
Guardians watch the world below.
Nature's shimmer, rich and bright,
Guides us through the dark of night.

The mountains stand, steadfast and tall,
Embracing echoes, ancient call.
In harmony with the earth's design,
Their presence gives the soul divine.

A world alive with spirit gleams,
The heart awakens, filled with dreams.
In the silence, nature sings,
The magical shimmer that life brings.

Nature's Glitter on a Brush of Green

On the canvas of the hills,
Nature paints with gentle thrills.
Emerald blades and poppy red,
Stories of the earth widespread.

Sunlight weaves through verdant threads,
Awakening the ground it spreads.
With every drop of dew it shares,
Nature's love in quiet prayers.

A brush of green where life abounds,
Whispers rising from the grounds.
Butterflies dance with graceful ease,
Nature's glitter in the breeze.

Amidst the wild and twinkling light,
Colors merge, a pure delight.
Each petal shimmers, soft and bright,
Nature's glitter, sheer respite.

In harmony, the flora sways,
Crafting joy in gentle ways.
A portrait framed by sky and earth,
Nature's brush, our endless worth.

Rhythms of Radiance in the Wild

In the wild, where echoes dance,
Nature hums a vibrant stance.
Every heartbeat, every sound,
A symphony that starts unbound.

Golden beams and silver streams,
Weaving through our waking dreams.
Rustling leaves and flowing air,
Craft a rhythm, free from care.

Mountains call with mighty grace,
Holding secrets, time can't erase.
Nature's rhythm, strong and free,
Beckons hearts to simply be.

Meadows sway to breezy tunes,
As stars awake in soft-lit moons.
In each moment, magic swells,
Rhythms of wild where freedom dwells.

Like a heartbeat, pure and clear,
Nature's whispers draw us near.
In the wild, we're never lost,
Radiance flows, whatever the cost.